The Book of Fair

Richard King, E. O. Hoppé

Alpha Editions

This edition published in 2021

ISBN : 9789355391131

Design and Setting By
Alpha Editions
www.alphaedis.com
Email - info@alphaedis.com

As per information held with us this book is in Public Domain.
This book is a reproduction of an important historical work. Alpha Editions uses the best technology to reproduce historical work in the same manner it was first published to preserve its original nature. Any marks or number seen are left intentionally to preserve its true form.

Beauty, Charm, & Beautiful Women the World Over

BEAUTY

"Beauty is only skin deep," cries Ugliness, pinning her faith on the fascination of the Intelligence. "And ugliness goes to the bone," Beauty replies, though she fears that that shaft of "wit" must have originally been spoken by a pantomime librettist. "Handsome is as handsome does," retorts Ugliness, quoting from the Plain Woman's volume of Copy-Book Maxims. And so this battle of words goes on.

But Beauty cares nothing at all for maxims. She puts on her most becoming hat, her daintiest dress, and goes forth careless and indifferent to anything except Middle Age. No shaft of Puritanical censure, she feels, can hurt her. Beauty is its own raison d'etre—its own excuse for being gloriously alive. It needs no apology, no panic balancing of its debit account by moral and intellectual compensations hurriedly placed to its credit. In Heaven, it knows, more people will want to call upon Ninon de l'Enclos than wish to leave cards on St. Theresa of Spain. And what is more satisfying to Beauty than a large audience? Only two things really terrify her—the loss of her Good Looks and the loss of her Youth. That may be the reason why, au fond, she sometimes envies her plainer sisters almost as much as they envy her. Perhaps she knows that they play a waiting game, and that at fifty-five it might have been as well for her had she been born "plain" too, since henceforward she must enter the "plain" woman's world as a stranger, to live as they live, but, unlike them, to be for ever tortured by the remark: "All the same, she was a great beauty *'In Her Day!'*" It is the way her friends apologize for her false teeth.

In the meanwhile, however, she triumphs—triumphs overwhelmingly. To the purely physical lure Reason is as unreasoning as Lunacy. In spite of that French saying which states that "il faut souffrir pour etre belle," how often great suffering and great happiness go through life hand in hand, the one utterly dependent upon the other. Only the commonplace "soul" revels in the smug security of the commonplace. Life at its fullest is surely a great joy, as well as a great pain!

And Beauty—how glibly we utter the word! Indeed, how glibly we utter all those words, the meaning of which is so difficult clearly to define! "Democracy," "Liberty," "Freedom," "Friendship," "Love"—and, let it be owned, the "Hereafter"!—how often we use the words as a kind of final argument, and how often, so mesmerized has become our Intelligence by these words, do we accept them without question as something appertaining to finality. It is the same with Beauty. To call a woman "beautiful" requires no corollary. That is all that need be said! Merely to say it, especially if the word is spoken by some one in High Authority, is sometimes sufficient to create a reputation for loveliness—as women who have been the mistresses of kings know full well. The world asks so little more of a beautiful woman than her beauty. Which perhaps accounts—though in a book of Beautiful Women let it be printed in small type—for so many lovely women being intellectually dull! But then, if one is good to look upon, one can afford to be dreary company. Loveliness is its own forgiveness of intellectual sins. It is a "decoration," and we do not ask of decorations to be more than perfect in regard to colouring and symmetry of line. Success is, after all, but a reflection of ourselves in the world, and Beauty finds its reflection in almost every human eye and in almost every human heart. Its way through life is indeed strewn with roses—those lovely flowers which hide such very vindictive thorns.

God makes beautiful women; a Plain Woman has to do the best she can for herself. Her only hope lies in the fact that what fascinates Tom may leave Dick indifferent—and who knows but that Harry will find that she herself is more attractive than any other woman? Which brings me back to a definition of Beauty, and that, being at heart a sluggard, I had purposely wished to avoid.

"Beauty" is to me but another name for "Harmony." It is harmonious to some ideal indigenous to the "soul." It may only be "skin deep," as the Plain Woman likes to assert for the benefit of vain schoolgirls, but the beholding eye nevertheless endows it with "spirituality." It likes to believe this loveliness is only an outer symbol of an inner spiritual grace. Which fact will account in some way for different types of beautiful women appealing to different types of men—so that even an ugly woman sometimes hears herself addressed in the language Mars probably used to Venus.

We find in Beauty something more than a realization of what we believe to be perfection; we find in it a "journey's end"—or perhaps I ought to say "lodgment," seeing that Beauty is so often fleeting—in the lonely search of the "soul" after spiritual sustenance. We give to it our adoration, an adoration which none the less overwhelms us emotionally because, physically speaking, it is passionless. We bow in worship before it, without—if I may express myself in metaphor tinged with vulgarity—an insensate desire to Clutch. For Beauty is also a "message"; and, as it appeals to something within our "souls," so does that "message" become the more eloquent. Moreover, it has a thousand facets. We can find it anywhere, in almost everything that is not mean or debased, hypocritical or dishonest. Nevertheless, there are some men who can find beauty only in sex; men who are deaf to that "song within a song" which in the hearts of so many is as the Psalm of Life. The view of distant mountains; the glowing, dancing reflection of the sun setting out at sea; the quiet, verdant valleys, whose peacefulness falls on the troubled spirit as a benediction; a voice, a memory, a prayer—all these things can uplift the heart until momentarily it may live in a whole world of beauty. For Beauty must be *felt* within the "soul." The senses but convey an impression, the "soul" translates that impression into terms of Ecstacy. For when we come face to face with Beauty, in whatever guise, all that is best and purest in our Nature stirs in response, so that at last our "soul" cannot live without Beauty. Robbed, as it were, for ever of this harmony, which seems to reflect Heaven, even in lowly places, it withers and dies. The man who seeks not Beauty can scarcely be said to live; since without beauty Life is but a barren wilderness, sodden by the tears of men. The Road to God is paved by Music and Poetry, by Art and Literature, by all those manifestations of Beauty which are unselfishness, renunciation, friendship, love, sympathy, understanding, humility. Man is Spirit as well as Body, and just as the physical needs must be satisfied, so must the Spirit find Beauty if it wither not nor die. Through Beauty God speaks to men; and inasmuch as we seek to bring Beauty into our lives and into the lives of others, so we come into closer communion with Him.

Beauty, then, is something which is in complete harmony with the longings of the "soul," and through the "soul" with God. The old belief that Beauty is the seed the Devil sows to reap his human harvest is an exploded blasphemy. Surround men with Ugliness and they will quickly qualify themseves for a place in Hell. We take from our surroundings as much, perhaps even more, than we give to them. Thus Beauty is surely the great ally of Virtue: to the extent that it sometimes fails in its alliance, so does it lack true perfection. For as much as our so-called civilization is worth to us in happiness, the gift has been a gift from the great poets, the great writers, the great thinkers, the great musicians and painters—all those who have sought to bring the message of beauty to this world, including that supreme artist Nature herself. And this is true, no matter how much the politicians, the commercial magnates, kings, princes, and potentates may preen themselves on their human importance, pointing to their laws, their factories, their palaces, all the evidences of their temporal power. Their "message" to humanity has only been the fact of their own success, whereas, the potent "message" of Beauty is at all times a silent one, though more eloquent, more uplifting, more encouraging than all the pompous diatribes that were ever uttered. In the greatest, most inspiring moments of our lives we are always dumb. No words can then express the triumphant melody which is surging in our hearts. To the extent that we can explain our emotion, so we feel it less. Thus in the presence of something beautiful we are at all times mute. The strength of its appeal is shown in our subsequent *ACTS*; and actions, we know, speak far, far louder than words.

Beauty, then, is something which, uplifting us, strengthens the soul, helps the spirit to rise above the deadening influence of the commonplace monotony of the Everyday. It may not necessarily be essential to our success in this world, though to surround oneself with Beauty is surely one of the ideals which spur us onward to the attainment of riches, but it is surely essential to our salvation! It is, as it were, the golden thread which runs through the plain homespun of life. Without it the pattern of our days would be distinctly "drab" on a buff ground. Everything that is physically fine; everything that is noble and just, generous and kind; everything which gladdens our hearts and sends us on our way rejoicing; everything which, as it were, lifts our faces up towards God in the high heavens—that surely is *Beautiful!* I always like to think that Shelley in his essay on "Love" made Love synonymous with Beauty: "Thou demandest what is Love?" he wrote. "It is that powerful attraction towards all that we conceive of fear, or hope beyond ourselves, when we find within our own thoughts the chasm of an insufficient void, and seek to awaken in all things that are, a community with what we experience within ourselves. If we reason, we would be understood; if we imagine, we would that the airy children of our brain were born anew within another's; if we feel, we would that another's nerves should kindle at once and mix and melt into our own, that lips of motionless ice should not reply to lips quivering and burning with the heart's best blood. This is Love. This is the bond and sanction which connects not only man with man, but with everything which exists."

To make the world more and more beautiful, not in a narrow sense, but in the widest and deepest sense possible, that surely ought to be the ideal of civilization. And in this ideal, physical beauty has surely an important place allotted to it. One is virtuous, after all, for one's own benefit; one "makes the best of oneself" for the benefit of the whole world. There is no virtue in being plain, though I must confess it usually makes virtue a much easier achievement. As a rule, Nature is more often a conscientious than an inspired artist, and there is nothing mere conscientiousness requires more than a helping hand. That conscientiousness has also its divinely inspired moments—moments which come to it unpremeditated and unforeseen— that also is a fad. That is why Nature, who "bungle" her best points hopelessly so often, does occasionally achieve a veritable "masterpiece." That, too, is why Beautiful Women have every reason to be proud of their loveliness and seek to preserve its colouring and its contour. Moreover, their beauty also absolves them from the necessity of being remarkable in any other direction. After all, if one is beautiful, it is not also obligatory to be useful. One does not demand of Leonardo da Vinci's "Mona Lisa" to be a screen as well as a picture, nor appreciate an exquisite piece of Sevres china any the less because it is also neither a candlestick nor an ash-tray! We demand from them nothing beyond their beauty, and, finding it, we are satisfied. Also we count our life worth while according to the loveliness which it contains. Every man starts out in the hope that he will marry a pretty woman. That most men's taste is not exacting, and love proverbially blind, is a blessing for which few lovers are sufficiently grateful. In the prayers of gratitude offered up by Humanity to God, such an one should be included: "Praise be unto Him who makes most of us beautiful at some time to some one!" Beauty is, after all, its own forgiveness of sins in the heart of those who love it. Only when a woman's looks are fading does her husband begin to realize that neither can she cook. Until then, he is only too glad to suffer indigestion at her hands. That a beautiful woman should die young is, after all, only to wish her the best of all possible blessings in this best of all possible worlds.

"As rich and purposeless as is the rose, Thy simple doom is to be beautiful."

All the same, what a pleasant destiny! And yet, perhaps, those who are permitted to gaze upon beauty without being themselves beautiful are the most fortunate of all. And that is the position of most of us, thank God. As it is more thrilling to watch a pageant than to take part in one, so, to be able to gaze undisturbed upon the Pageant of Beauty as it passes before our generation to take its place in the wonderful procession marching down the ages, is a far more peaceful proceeding than to form part of that procession. After all, the most envied in a tableau vivant are not those who figure in it, but those who have been able to secure the best position from which to view it. The man who secures a "masterpiece" is far more gratified than the artist who created it. So, while we bow down in adoration before Beauty, let us also be thankful that the greatest privilege of all lies in an opportunity to regard it. "Beauty and sadness," George Macdonald has written, "always go together." But to be able to gaze on Beauty—that, surely, is the most undiluted joy in life.

CHARM

Almost every woman believes that, though Nature may not have made her beautiful, of her own accord she can achieve charm. "Charm" is the Possibility which Desire dangles before the nose of Hope. And every woman, who *is* a woman endeavours to make that Possibility a Certainty once, at least, in her life. To be beautiful is a great deal, but to be charming is of greater value and infinitely less dangerous to one's peace of mind. Especially to know that one is irresistible to some one whom one has no particular desire to resist—that surely is *everything*! What, then, *is* Charm?

Artemus Ward described a charming woman as "born to make hash of men's buzzoms"—which, though comprehensive, does not lead us very far, and sounds perilously near being a cooking recipe. Oscar Wilde said: "All charming people, I fancy, are spoiled. It is the secret of their attraction"— which, personally, I disbelieve absolutely. Spoiled people manage to get their own way, it is true, since the majority of us are so faint-hearted that we find it easier to offer ourselves in sacrifice than play our part in a scène à faire. But the effect of a metaphorical foot on one's neck is by no means a satisfying sensation, though we may endure it heroically. Longfellow described a charming woman as "when she passed it seemed like the ceasing of exquisite music," and this, though pleasing to the ear, seems to say so much and mean as little as any modern drawing-room ballad. Shakespeare, perhaps, came nearer giving us a word-picture of Charm when he wrote: "She told him stories to delight his ear; she showed him favours to allure his eye"; but even that description does not convey to us much more than the effort of a cook to fascinate a policeman. Charm is something more subtle than the ability to tell a smoking-room story in a drawing-room way and exhibit the best "points" Nature has given us with a fine semblance of doing so unconsciously. Perhaps the Dictionary gives the best definition when it explains Charm as being "something possessing occult power or influence." Occultism seems the easiest explanation of the personal "sway" which some outwardly unattractive person wields over the most unlikely people, people who, by all reason and logic, policy and prudence, ought not to be thus fascinated. Love is easier to explain than Charm; or rather, perhaps, I ought to add, than that emotion which so often passes muster for Love, that emotion which, though it often ends in marriage, or divorce, or a six-months' despair, may arise from no more solid foundation than solitude, a moonlight night, and the sex-appeal of two people in a "romantic" mood. But just as Time is the supreme test of Love, so it is also the supreme test of Charm. A woman who is as charming at forty-nine as she was, say, at thirty, must necessarily possess something inherent in her nature, not recognizable as "beauty" perchance, which leads men nevertheless—and, what is infinitely more difficult, other *women*— by a single hair. Charm, indeed, has nothing whatever to do with either beauty or youth. Its genius lies in being able to delude the world that it is both beautiful as well as youthful, no matter what adverse criticism artists may indulge in, nor how many cold, ugly facts Father Time may bring forward to dispel the illusion. Real Charm rises superior to both. It is a quality which, because it cannot be analysed, cannot therefore be destroyed. So it is easier to call it "Occult," which the Dictionary informs us is a power "hidden from the eye and understanding." On the other hand, perhaps, it may be an unconscious form of *mesmerism*, the mesmerist being as totally unaware of his gift as the mesmerised is of his power.

But if we cannot break up Charm into its component parts, we can, at least, say definitely what it is not. It cannot be cultivated, for one thing, though life and experience may help to make it finer, more exquisite. Nor is it necessarily the natural possession of either beautiful or clever people. Most of us have met men and women who were both mediocre in appearance and uncultivated in mind, who nevetheless were charming in no slight degree, in that the evidence of charm be admiration and friendship. The natural gift they possessed was the power to make all those with whom they came in contact *feel charming* too, and this, after all, may or may not be the great secret of Charm? Beauty is delightful to gaze upon; but it is, as it were, a self-contained quality—we cannot share in it except as spectators. But the genius of a charming man or woman is that they help to bring out all that is best in other people. Beauty only makes other people feel more beautiful or infinitely plainer and either is a very lonely feeling. But in Charm we seem to share; it seems to mingle us, not only with the charmer, but with all the world around them. Beauty is like a wonderful jewel; but Charm, if I may refer to it in metaphor, resembles an ideal home. And who would not rather pawn their jewellery than break up a happy domesticity? It is perhaps this feeling which Charm gives us of being perfectly "at home" that is its most precious possession. So, may be, it is really the one word we give to that quality of the mind and heart which mingles both sympathy and understanding in equal quantities. Most women, when they desire to cultivate Charm, read up the Memoirs of Ninon de l'Enclos, whereas they would be much wiser to analyze the attractive qualities of the dog! Animals are always charming, because they are always natural; and to be *natural* is ninety per cent of fascination. The reason so many men and women are bores is because so many men and women are never content to make the best of what they are, but are always pretending to be what they are not, generally ending their performance by giving a dismal caricature of the Ideal they have tried so vainly to emulate. Even honesty in this world of masks is charming. I don't, of course, mean that honesty which will scrupulously repay threepenny bits, but the honesty which will be content to be exactly what it is, without pretence or disguise, and with no additional trimming in the way of either gold lace or sackcloth and ashes. An artificial person is never charming, though they may sometimes achieve a charming effect. An honest wrongdoer is infinitely more attractive than a Saint who pretends that he has done no wrong. The great charm of a charming person is that he can mingle the most diverse human elements, bringing them down to the one common denominator of Humanity, where all that is true in Nature forges that link which binds men together in brotherhood and humility. Charm pierces all disguise: its influence is so delightful, since it helps us to be our true selves, repriving us for the nonce from that effort of "pretending" which the world expects to find, and is embarrassed when this expectation fails. Charm, then, is not a gift like Beauty, but a grateful acceptance, unconsciously illustrating in our hearts the fact that it is more satisfying to *give* than to receive. In this way the Loquacious finds a good Listener most attractive, and the Strong are never so happy with themselves as when administering to the needs of the Weak. Two "born talkers" were born to hate each other; just as one good listener finds another good listener exceedingly dull company. That, too, is why Reserve thinks Vivacity a thing of infinite repose, and the Vivacious discover in the Reserved a silent strength more inspiring than eloquence. It is the man or woman whose gifts bring out all the best in us who we call "charming," since further description seems unnecessary. Charming people, then, must perforce be *natural*, since artificiality raises between men a bulwark which not even Good Intentions can scale. They must also be sympathetic, since those who demand sympathy are rarely more than tolerated. They must also possess "Understanding," since without Understanding one might as well reveal oneself to a brick wall. Granted these things, it will not take us very long to find them beautiful as well.

Charm is not, then, an *assertive* quality, unless unselfishness can resemble "assertiveness." Rather is it the power to draw from others those natural qualities which otherwise lie dormant within them. We all yearn to be our true selves: the difficulty is that we receive so little encouragement from those with whom we are brought into contact. Thus, as I wrote before, we are all apt to find charm in those who, as it were, seem to possess the key to our hearts. We delight to talk to them, because with them we feel safe from that danger which besets us so often—the danger of being wilfully misunderstood, wilfully misjudged, our "dreams" and "ideals" wilfully distorted. In their society we expand, living and speaking as free men would live and speak in a world of real freedom. Leaving them to return to the world is as a "farewell" to liberty upon re-entering prison. Physically they may not attract us; though, such is the potency of Charm, that those we like we very soon begin to admire. Which is a blessing without the least disguise, since it enables those who have neither youth nor beauty nor wealth to recommend them to find friendship and love nevertheless. Charm is, as it were, the passion of a "soul"—a passion in which there is nothing physical, but rather a mental and spiritual elation overwhelming the simple "call of the flesh." Thus real Charm is ageless, because it can triumph even over physical decay. The Charm of Innocence; the Charm of Youth;—these states do not really belong to those gifts of sympathy and understanding which are the two chief elements of Charm. Youth and Innocence leave us at last. Our regret over their departure is at best a purely academic sorrow. In the hearts of those who find us charming we know that we can defy Age. Our greater Knowledge will but give us a clearer Understanding, and for these things shall we be loved. Charm, in fact, is what maturity offers men and women in exchange for their Youth. In finding it, they escape that loneliness which is the one haunting terror of growing old. We speak, of course, of "charming girls" and "charming young men," but what we really mean is that they are merely nice and young. "Charming," indeed, is a word which we use as thoughtlessly as we use "Love." We employ it to express prettiness and elegance, daintiness and good-nature. But none of these things necessarily express "Charm" any more than do those couples, who make use of the trees in Hyde Park to cuddle beneath them, express Love. They are just words we employ because our Dictionary is limited and we cannot think of any other. Real Charm is something much more subtle than any of these things—more subtle, yet more potent. In fact, no one may pride themselves on the possession of Charm until Time has robbed them of all those "minor beauties." Indeed, if I were asked to explain Charm—and in thus being asked I should be faced by the difficulty of explaining the well-nigh inexplicable— I should sum it up as a kind of *super-intelligence of the* "soul," an intelligence which combines the wisdom of the Heart with the wisdom of the World, the Wisdom of the Serpent with some of the guileless optimism of the Dove; above all, the gift of interpreting men and women to themselves, thus bringing to their troubled "souls" that sense of repose which comes from an opportunity to be completely natural, and, in being natural, to arise refreshed in body and spirit, ready for further efforts to solve the problem of true Happiness in Life.

Beautiful Women the World Over

In the preceding pages I have tried to explain my belief that Beauty is some quality from which we seek inspiration, and that Charm is that natural gift which helps us to give inspiration to others. When Beauty is combined with Charm—a rarer combination than Society papers would lead us to believe—you have that quality, akin to genius, which has made a few beautiful women stand out, bold figures, in the long history of the world.

In olden days, when monarchs were wont to wield their sceptres rather in the manner of a bomb-thrower his bombs, it was sufficient for a woman to attract the Royal eye for her at once to gain the reputation of world-wide beauty. Royal mistresses were always lovely ipso facto. It was lése majesté to dispute the Royal taste in feminine beauty. All the same, as one gazes nowadays upon these sirens of a past age, one confesses to oneself that most monarchs set out on their voyages à Cythère in very rudely constructed barques. Instinctively, however, we still try to see these ladies through Royal eyes, praising them accordingly. Maybe our professed admiration for them is all part and parcel of that glamour which we weave, even to-day, around our "lesser" terrestrial deities. A lady mayoress still shares with duchesses the genius of always smiling "graciously." (Until such a time, of course, as, her husband being denied re-election, we designate those signs of amiability on her part merely as varieties of the much-reviled "grin.")

In this the Twentieth Century the aesthetic taste of monarchs is no longer approved unquestioningly by all the world. The power of a King's mistress is at present more social than aesthetic. To-day the photographer is more potent in the creation of a woman's reputation for beauty than the most autocratic emperor. Photography is no longer merely the business of exact reproduction—it is an Art, penetrating in its psychological illustration of character. As one gazes at those depressing likenesses of lovely women who lived sixty years ago, one realizes at once the popularity of such painters as Winterhalter. He, at any rate, made his "sitters" look like half-sisters to the Empress Eugenie, in a pose designed expressly for the decoration of a chocolate box. To-day the photographer has usurped the position of all but the greatest portrait-painters. And this, for the reason that the best modern photographers must also of necessity be artists. They must undergo something of the same rigorous training as painters. It is no longer a question of a good camera, a studio, and the exhibition case of "samples" hung outside the front door. A modern photographer must understand all the nuances of light and shade, tone value, colour, pose, proportion. His studies must have the characteristics of first-class paintings—minus, of course, their colour. Nevertheless, this omission must be suggested through the variations of light and shade. It is because Mr. Hoppé is also a painter that the reproductions in this book are so superb in all those details which go to make up perfection in portraiture. They are not merely photographs (as we in our ignorance often designate photography as "mere"). They represent an art nearly akin to the finest portrait painting. Note, for example, the exquisite manner in which light and shade has been employed to throw into relief just those most lovely features which each face possesses individually, even the most beautiful. Note especially in this regard how cleverly the artist has caught the different characteristics which belong to each individual nationality—the Red Indian type of beauty, for example, as contrasted with that of the English. The difference is not so marked in the contour of the face, nor in the features, but in the *eyes*. There you have a whole volume of comparisons. Those of the Red Indian Beauty, exquisite in their shape, seem nevertheless to have, as it were, a shutter closed down behind them. They are unfathomable. The typical English eyes, on the other hand, how clear they are, how open; how we seem able to see right into them—deep down into the labyrinth of thought! Examine the Spanish portrait, and note how cleverly the artist has thrown into relief those most lovely characteristics of Spanish beauty—the formation of the chin, the eyebrows, the fascinating manner in which the hair is arranged as a framework for the modelling of the whole face. The Gipsy beauty—how admirably it shows the wayward grace of the Gipsy race; its wide and open countenance, suggestive of life led in the free air; the characteristic eyes, with their hint of Asiatic origin. Take also the picture of a typical Italian beauty—in this case Neapolitan in type. Even in this photograph one can almost see that blue-black tint so beautiful in the hair of Italian women. Note, too, the perfect Roman profile, the lovely upper lip, the sensitive nostrils—all so suggestive of a nation in which emotion and feeling are rarely suppressed. The Russian beauty—how attractive and how typical she is! Note the almost square jaw, the sensuous mouth, the upper eyelid slightly overhanging—a characteristic which lends to Russian women that unique fascination which belongs to the "language of the eye." Indeed, it may be said that a Russian woman can express herself by her eyes alone, whereas an English woman *talks*, and yet is often misunderstood.

In discussing these portraits with Mr. Hoppé he revealed to me a somewhat unconventional belief—his belief that, in America, there is no such thing as a "typical American face." Every type is represented over there, and no one predominates over another. American women differ from English women in a certain native "chic," approaching almost to the instinctive grace of the French woman; a certain intellectual "flair"; a "liveliness"—if I may so express it—all typical of a mixed race, still young enough to be content to imitate unconsciously the type it most admires, and being able to do so since it possesses the inherited characteristics of so many different nationalities.

This book gives us a wonderful example of representative French beauty. Note the mouth—how typical it is! The perfect poise of the head on the neck; the equally beautiful throat and shoulders. Moreover, this portrait is especially interesting, since it shows us how lovely white hair can be as the framework of a still youthful face.

To contrast the Chinese and Japanese beauties is also interesting. There is a gentle sweetness about the Japanese face which is undoubtedly appealing; but it does not compare in character with that of the Chinese lady. The contour of the Chinese face, though less round, has a straighter nose, the modelling of every feature is firmer, infinitely less flaccid. It is interesting, too, to compare the Cuban beauty with that of the Hawaiian. The latter type is less classical; there is a stronger influence of the negro in it. Indeed, the Hawaiian type of beauty may be described as being only just far enough removed from the negro to be pretty. In the Cuban woman the nose is more classically modelled; the whole contour of the face nearly resembles that of the European. Even in Western eyes she possesses charm.

One hardly knows how to admire the Portuguese type of beauty. It is undoubtedly striking—though, if I may so express it, the model chosen by Mr. Hoppé seems too unapproachable to make any facile appeal. It is, however, interesting in this portrait to observe traces of the Spanish type, combined with an undoubtedly Moorish influence as seen in the way the eyes are set in the face. The eyes, indeed, are the most fascinating part of the picture. Regard them well, they are uncanny; they are almost unreal. I have seen eyes like that in crudely carved wooden idols—so primitive in their modelling, yet so extraordinarily expressive in their regard: *seeing* eyes with, as it were, an impenetrable blind drawn close down behind them, shutting out thought. If not the most strictly beautiful, this Portuguese type is one of the most psychologically *interesting* in the whole pageant of this book of beauty.

And yet, how attractive in their variety all these faces are! Could anything be more alluring than the lovely eyes, the perfectly shaped mouth of the Chilian beauty, a beauty also strongly characteristic of the Spanish type? How lovely, too, is the Greek face, with the nose, as it were, a deliberate continuation of the forehead. There is passion and grace in the Indian woman, with her lovely supple body, the expression of melancholy in her face, those exquisite velvet eyes the size of which seem almost completely to dwarf the other features!

Among such a galaxy of lovely women each man may surely find one who represents to him his physical ideal. The charm of these portraits is that each beautiful woman, typical of her race, possesses some unique beauty which belongs to her nationality alone. In each face there is a charm which more than compensates us for its deviation from the characteristics we, as

Englishmen, most especially admire. He must be prejudiced indeed in favour of one type who can deny a certain loveliness to any one of them.

Very few there will surely be malcontent to leave this book to posterity as a portrait-gallery of some of the loveliest women representative of the world of our day. Naturally, there are other beautiful women in the world who are not included. This is one book—not a whole library! But who will dispute the right of those who do appear therein? No one—surely!

And, after all, were a Martian suddenly to descend to Earth and demand of us representatives of the finest examples of the Human Race, should we not parade before him our most beautiful women?

RICHARD KING

1922

Thirty-two Portraits

1. AMERICA—Lady Lavery

2. AMERICA—Mrs. Lydig Hoyt

3. AMERICA—Viscountess Maidstone

4. AMERICA—Miss Malvina Longfellow

5. AMERICA—Miss Marion Davies

6. RED INDIAN—Princess White Deer

7. ENGLAND—"Hebe"

8. ENGLAND—Lady Diana Duff-Cooper

9. ENGLAND—Miss Gladys Cooper

10. ENGLAND—Miss Kathlene Martyn

11. SCOTLAND—Viscountess Masserene and Ferrard

12. IRELAND—Miss Grace D'Arcy

13. FRANCE—Mlle. Raymonde Thuillier

14. ALGIERS—Madame Revalles

15. SPAIN—Señora Tortola Valencia

16. GIPSY—Miss Fedora Roselli

17. ITALY—Signora Comanetti

18. PORTUGAL—Señora Maria Di Castellani

19. RUSSIA—Mlle. Fedorova

20. POLAND—Madame Mika Mikun

21. NORWAY—Miss Olga Morrison

22. SWEDEN—Miss Anna Q. Nillson

23. ARMENIA—Armen Ter Ohanian

24. CHILE—Countess Lisburne

25. ECUADOR—Mrs. Haddon Chambers

26. INDIA—Princess Monchsa

27. JAPAN—Mrs. Tokugawa

28. CHINA—Mrs. Wellington Koo

29. CUBA

30. HAITI

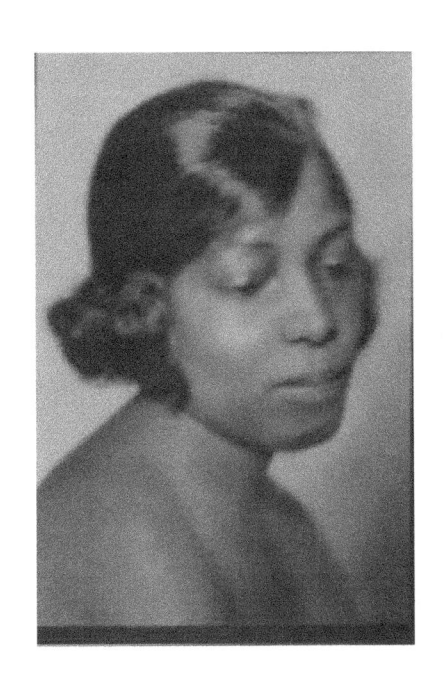

31. HAWAI

32. DUTCH WEST INDIES

www.ingramcontent.com/pod-product-compliance
Ingram Content Group UK Ltd.
Pitfield, Milton Keynes, MK11 3LW, UK
UKHW040844230425
5580UKWH00016B/668

9 789355 391131